Really Really

Heaps and Heaps

Really Really
Heaps and Heaps

HANNAH PFISTER

Really Really Heaps and Heaps
by Hannah Pfister
© 2025 by Ellerslie Press

ISBN 978-1-943592-88-3

Ellerslie Press
Windsor, CO

Published in the United States of America.

To Joe who taught me to count from the Right.
To Adam, because without him I would still be
Hannah Hannah Bobanna. And to the Ludy Boys who
convinced me that the book manuscript I wrote in
1994 ought to actually be published.

Contents

A Note From the Author

This manuscript was written at a defining juncture in my life in June of 1994. I originally typed it into an old word processing program on my old Commodore XT. Although that computer has long since bitten the dust, a printout of my writing was preserved in an old storage box found in my basement — yellowed, severely water damaged, and barely legible in parts. The Ludy Boys swung by to visit me this past year and asked me if I would be willing to write down my story of "life with Joe Hardy." That is when I remembered this manuscript. Freshly inspired, I rummaged around in the basement for a couple of days and finally found the manuscript. What you have before you is basically, except for a few small grammatical adjustments, the way I wrote it when I was twenty-six years old, newly married, with two young children. I'm not as young now, have been happily married for thirty-five years, and have five grandchildren and counting. There have been many tears shed in the re-reading and re-typing of this manuscript. God gave me a very precious gift when he gave me Joe Hardy. Because of it, I'm convinced to this day that Christ loves me — really really heaps and heaps. I hope reading this story blesses you as much as living it did me.

Ever-counting from the *Right*,

Hannah Pfister

April 5, 2025

Counting from the Left

I started out my life with the name Hannah Hunter. Then through adoption, I became Hannah Hardy. And through marriage, I became Hannah Pfister.

Three names, three completely different Hannahs.

Hannah Hunter was emotionally abused by others — a victim.

Hannah Hardy was an emotional abuser — a victimizer.

Hannah Pfister? Well, she is an entirely different story.

It's Saturday, June 18, in the year 1994 as I sit down to write this book.

I hate to admit it, but Adam and I were glued to the television set last night watching (along with ninety-five million other dumb Americans) the Los Angeles police and media helicopters chase a white Ford Bronco down the 405 freeway in Southern California.

The strange event lasted a few hours and involved a man named O. J. Simpson. Supposedly he's famous. I personally had never heard of him until last night when all this went down.

From what I can gather, O. J. Simpson is accused of some really bad crimes, and he was asked by the Los Angeles Police Department to turn himself in yesterday. But he wasn't interested in turning himself in, so he hopped into his white Ford Bronco and fled. And like a social conformist, I was transfixed.

This morning, sitting here to write this book, I'm embarrassed to admit that last night I skipped my women's Bible study, failed to get dinner on the table for my family, and wasted my entire evening watching this uneventful slow-speed chase.

The reason I'm starting out this book with this piece of information is to practice being honest with you. I know better than to turn on the television set during the dinner hour. I know better than to be drawn into harebrained human dramas just because the media wishes me to. And I know better than to drag others into the unnecessary drama right along with me. I admit that it was entirely my fault that my husband was unprepared for his Saturday men's breakfast this morning, and my two darling children were cranky and in need of a bit of extra TLC to start out the day today.

It was all *my* fault.

You don't know me well enough to realize how revolutionary that statement is coming out of my mouth.

For the first twenty-something years of my life, I doubt I had ever taken responsibility for a single bad decision or errant action I had made.

It was all *their* fault.

That was the statement you could expect to hear coming out of my mouth. In my mind, my problems were the result of others, not me.

Playing the victim may seem at first to be the easier road through life, but it comes with some unexpected potholes. Potholes, mind you, that totally destroy your tires and your suspension, and ultimately cause your entire engine to dislodge from your vehicle.

My problem?

I grew up counting from the *Left*.

My parents *left* me when I was eight. Both of them in one week. First my dad left my mother. Then my mother left me.

My Aunt Phyllis reluctantly took me in after that. That arrangement lasted two years until Aunt Phyllis realized that I was holding her back — cramping her style. So one morning I left for school and came back home in the afternoon to a locked apartment. I never saw Aunt Phyllis again. She *left* me, just like my parents had.

I spent the next six miserable years in the foster system.

When I was thirteen, believe it or not, I was arrested for arson — for burning down a house on Mulberry Street. I did a lot of dumb things growing up, but, ironically, I didn't actually do *this* dumb thing. It was Kenny, my low-life fifteen-year-old boyfriend, who actually did the deed. But I was the one that eyewitness Charlie testified having spotted at the scene, so they tagged me with the crime.

At the time this happened, I had two bosom friends, Gem and Katie. On the Friday night following the fire, I was enjoying a slumber party at Gem's house with both of them when Katie's parents called Gem's parents and passed along the awful news of Hannah Hunter's purported dirty deed. I vividly remember Gem's mom handing me the telephone. On the other end was my foster mom, Trina.

"Hannah," Trina had said, "you are going to need to come home and sleep here tonight. Mike is on his way right now to pick you up."

Gem, Katie, and I were all in Gem's large rec room watching *The Ghosts of Buxley Hall* when the phone call happened. As I talked to Trina on the phone in the rec room, Gem's mom asked Gem and Katie to come with her. They left me all alone in the rec room to wait for Mike to arrive ten minutes later. I remember the movie still playing in the background as I fought back tears. Gem and Katie *left* me. I never talked with them again.

Being *left* was an art form I had learned to master when young.

Left was the dominant direction of my life. Everyone I cared about *left*. And so when I counted in life, I counted from the *Left*. One — my parents *left*. Two — Aunt Phyllis *left*. Three — my best friends *left*. Three *Lefts*. Three compelling reasons to reinforce my position as a victim. Three wonderful supporting arguments for the fact that all my problems were a direct result of other people's issues.

When Joe Hardy adopted me at the age of sixteen, I was a wreck. I was an angry, hurting mess.

Every time I faced difficulty, I freshly counted my three *Lefts*. One, two, three. I sucked on them like they were a baby's pacifier. I would darkly ponder how hard my life was, and how all my pain was someone else's fault.

I wanted the love of a father more than anything in all of life. But then when Joe Hardy loved me as a father, I rejected his love. Why? Because all I could think about was how painful it was going to be when I would need to count yet another *Left* in my life. When he too would decide to leave.

If three *Lefts* were doing me in, what would the emotional fall-out be if I were forced to count yet another?

Yesterday, the Los Angeles Police Department summoned O. J. Simpson to surrender himself to the authorities.

But he was scared. He didn't want to give up. So he hopped into his white Ford Bronco and tried to get away.

As I watched that white Bronco navigate its way down the 405 freeway at thirty miles an hour surrounded by police cars, I couldn't help but feel that that was my life.

God was saying, "Hannah, my child. Please surrender."

But I was scared. I didn't want to give up the little control I still possessed. So I chugged down the 405 for twenty years of my life in a chase that had a foregone conclusion.

It's a beautiful and wonderful thing to be chased down the 405 freeway of life by the Almighty Creator.

Even when I was at my ugliest and most unlovely state, my God saw me...and loved me. He turned on the flashing lights and set out to win me.

I'm just so happy that He's better at winning me than I am at running from Him.

Chapter One

Uncle Hal

Uncle Hal, my birth mother's oldest brother, was a scoundrel.

He would swindle you out of your last nickel if he could. Before he died at the age of fifty, he had spent more years in prison than out of it.

Even though I only met him once when I was nine, he has always been the embodiment to me of "The Old Bearded Con Man."

As I mentioned in my introduction, I have always struggled with being "the victim." I hate being the victim, but it's a deep-seated habit in my soul. It's my go-to place when the winds of difficulty start to gust in my life.

I've tried to describe the logic behind "being a victim" to my husband, Adam. Since "self-pity" is not something that Adam has ever really struggled with, he doesn't really get what motivates someone to go to this particular place when things go south in their life.

"Why wouldn't you choose to go to a happy place when things are sad?" he asks, genuinely perplexed. "Why would you go into a deep dungeon, stick on chains, and sit in an inch of frigid water?"

Good question. I wish I had a reasonable answer.

The best illustration I've been able to come up with so far is Uncle Hal and the Old Bearded Con Man Ruse.

The Old Bearded Con Man Ruse goes like this:

I'm walking down Franklin Avenue in Mayfield on a hot July day — sweating profusely. I would really like to cool off. That is when Uncle Hal shows up.

"Hannah, sweetie," he croons, "have I got just the thing for you!"

He points down at some very wet and deep concrete right off the sidewalk I'm journeying down.

"Step right in here, missy," he says. "It's cool and comfortable in there. It'll even detoxify your feet and get rid of that foot odor you've been struggling with.

"But isn't that concrete?" I question with grave concern. "Won't it harden? Won't I get stuck?"

"Hogwash!" he replies. "Who told you such nonsense? Concrete hardens, but not quickly. You can get the cooling and detoxifying benefits from this lovely mixture, and then step out and be on your way in no time. What do you say?"

"Are you sure it's safe?" I ask.

"Have I ever lied to you before?" he replies.

Yes. In fact, he's never told me the truth. And, like the dupe I am, I step off the clear path home and right into Uncle Hal's Foot Cooling Elixir...only to find that I'm immediately stuck when I do. Uncle Hal, recognizing that I've listened to his nonsense yet again, grabs my purse, yanks off my necklace, and even runs off with my pretty pearl earrings. And you know why? Because he's a liar and a thief.

Every time I played the victim growing up it was

just like that. Uncle Hal would promise me satisfaction, revenge, justice, or consolation, and I would buy it. And the next thing you know I'd be breathing into a brown paper bag with an anxiety attack.

Uncle Hal was always offering something my soul wanted, but he never actually gave it to me.

Let it be noted in this first chapter, Uncle Hal is a scoundrel.

Many of you reading this have an invisible Uncle Hal in your life too. I hope and pray my personal battle with overcoming Uncle Hal's nonsense will prove helpful to your own future victory.

Chapter Two

Hannah Hannah Bobanna

Candy Muggins was my best friend when I was fifteen. If there are good friends and bad friends, she would definitely land in the bad friend category.

Candy and I had a lot in common. We were both foster kids, we were both extremely troubled, and we both loved to blame everyone else in our life for our miseries.

I don't know that my year with Candy was the darkest point in my life, but it was possibly the most defining. It established a very clear "Uncle Hal always dupes me" motif in my life. I call it my Hannah Hannah Bobanna season. That is the name Candy called me almost exclusively for that one awful year. And still to this day, when I hear that name, I feel the agony of that time period — I feel small, weak, rejected, and like I'm a rebel teenager all over again.

In June of 1983 I was taken in by the Carlisle family. In late August of that year I started at a new school in Lake City. For the entirety of that year I lived dangerously on the edge of total self-destruction.

Candy and I made for a nasty pair. We were mean to anyone who was nice to us. We were terrifying to anyone who was mean to us.

We schemed about how we could steal, how we could find drugs, how we could entice boys, and how we could get back at the foster system that had so injured us.

Jim and Mary Carlisle were really nice people. But, with the help of Candy, I made sure they regretted the day they decided to give me a home.

Candy and I would meet together after school every day under the bridge on the east side of town. That was our base for our insidious, conspiratorial operations.

"We should get back at 'em," Candy would say.

"How?" I would ask. "I can't get caught. The social worker said that if I do one more thing, I'm headed to juvee."

"It's easy," Candy would smile. "You make it look like someone else is responsible."

We ran devious covert operations for that whole year. And just like I was once blamed for lowlife Kenny's arson, we tagged kids all over Lake City with petty crimes and misdemeanors that they didn't actually commit.

For instance, we got back at Sandy Kiegel for her dirty look during gym class by planting Mrs. Taylor's grade book in her locker. Mark Rogers spent an entire day in the police station thanks to the threatening letter we wrote using his name. And Marcy Campbell rued the day she took Candy's seat in biology class. We stowed Mr. Hendrick's class gerbil in her gym bag.

We nailed Jimmy Driscoll for his horrible "fatso" remark about Candy by throwing a baseball through Principle Joyner's window with Jimmy's name scribbled on the outside of it. The plan didn't really work — ultimately betrayed by Candy's girly handwriting of the name "Jimmy" — but it sure did make Jimmy's life miserable for a couple days.

There were probably ten other schemes like these that we attempted to pull off. Some worked, some didn't.

But without question, our most disgusting scheme was when we attempted to get back at Jim and Mary Carlisle for not allowing me to go out with Candy to the mall one Saturday afternoon.

I hate to even admit the crime, but I think it is important for you to truly understand the depths of depravity from which God has lifted me.

Candy and I, in the dead of night, took two pink spray paint bottles and spray painted the front of the Carlisle house with the word *Nazis!*

We dropped a business card from Chad Ryle, a moppy-haired kid who managed the local pet and feed store on Lincoln Street. We thought he looked like the sort who might do something sketchy like that.

It worked...at least at first. The Carlisles were sickened by the whole affair and pressed charges against Chad Ryle while Candy and I gloated over our successful career in the business of revenge.

And somewhere in the middle of the drama, I felt something that I hadn't really ever felt before. Guilt. Intense guilt.

Looking back, I realize it was God's way of waking me up. But I wasn't ready to wake up. So I buried this intense guilt by counting from the *Left*. I stepped into Uncle Hal's wet concrete and got freshly stuck in a state of victimhood.

But the reason I share this story is because of what happened next. About three weeks after the spray paint incident, Candy was arrested for stealing her foster parents' car. She was brought into the police station and, for whatever reason, told them all the things she and I had cooked up over the previous year.

The police called Jim and Mary that very day to let them know about Candy's confession, and I discovered what wrath looks like. Jim was irate and Mary was ready to scratch my eyes out. The hate, the anger, and the intense heat of emotion were nearly overwhelming to me. These two sweet humans turned on me and kicked me out of their lives. That very night social services took me from the Carlisle home and turned me over to the police.

The wrath, the hatred, the resentment, and the rejection the Carlisles shoved in my direction was totally reasonable. I was terrible and their response was justified. It's what I deserved. But, though I deserved it, it didn't help me change. It only helped reinforce the notion that I was easy to reject, easy to disdain, and easy to throw out with the trash. It made me all the more susceptible to the Old Bearded Con Man Ruse.

The thought of experiencing yet another *Left* in my life was nearly suffocating. At all costs, I couldn't go through such pain again.

Chapter Three

The Threat of Adoption

I spent five weeks in juvenile detention in 1984 after the Carlisle incident. And then one day in August, Samantha, my gruff detention officer walked up to me and said, "Pick up your things, Hunter. You're out."

"I'm out?" I said. "I thought I had three months."

"The judge made an exception," Samantha said.

"Where am I going?" I asked.

"Some dude's adopting you," she said matter-of-factly.

The entire thing sounded strange and bizarre. I was sixteen, almost seventeen, and some random guy was suddenly adopting me? There was no advance notice, no warning, no nothing. Just "some dude's adopting you"!

First of all, "dudes" don't adopt. Families adopt. Maybe a single woman might adopt. But not "dudes."

"Some dude's adopting you." Samantha's words echoed through my mind on repeat.

I was a foster kid, a criminal, a reject — worthless trash. So it's not that I felt I deserved better. It's not that

I expected a choice in the matter. In fact, I had never had a choice. But this situation riled me up.

I didn't like juvee, but at least I knew what to expect there. The thought of "being adopted" sounded like a wonderful way to get hurt again. I could feel the pending rejection, the future pain associated with such a forward step — it was oppressive.

I asked for an emergency meeting with Mrs. Inchin, the senior program officer.

"Hannah Hunter?" she said raising an eyebrow. "Why are you here? I thought you were heading out."

"About that," I said, "Is it already like…um…final?"

"What do you mean?" she said, confused.

"Am I already adopted?" I asked. "Mrs. Inchin, please! I don't want to go."

"Are you crazy, girl?" she replied. "You wish to stay here in detention instead of becoming a part of a family?"

"Yes," I answered.

She looked at me for a while attempting to figure out what was really going on.

"Look," she said, "this is a really good situation for you. I know your last placement was rough, but I strongly believe this one could be different."

"Mrs. Inchin," I said, "could you please help me? I don't want…to go."

Being a lousy foster child with a criminal record doesn't afford you a lot of pull in the system. Mrs. Inchin was convinced that this "dude" was going to prove to be an amazing father for me. She was convinced that he was positioned to give me opportunities that I likely never would get otherwise. So whether I wanted this or not, it was moving forward. I was being formally adopted.

In hindsight, I realize Mrs. Inchin was right. Hannah Hunter needed to become Hannah Hardy if she was ever going to stop counting from the *Left*.

As I was leaving juvenile detention that day in August 1984, I had no idea what an astounding, life-transforming adventure lay just up ahead.

Chapter Four

Meeting Joe Hardy

I was sitting in a counseling room with Monica, my social worker, at a YMCA in Denver, Colorado, when I first met Joe Hardy.

I fidgeted with the keychain on my backpack, stood up and sat back down, paced around the small room and kept saying over and over again to Monica, "I don't want this! I don't want this!"

"Just shut up and be a good girl" was the great advice Monica offered.

What was I doing in that waiting room?

I was counting from the *Left*. Over and over again in my mind I was thinking about my hurts, my aches, my bruises, and my pains. Uncle Hal was stealing everything from me while my feet were hardened in the concrete of self-pity.

Then, right in the middle of my saying, "Monica, I don't want this!" — he walked in through the door.

With a smile that stretched across the entire room and a personality so big the room seemed to glow yellow, Joe Hardy strode into my life.

"Howdy, princess!" he shouted as he lumbered into the

room. He came straight at me. I froze in terror, then he hugged me with the single most powerful hug I'd ever experienced.

"Oh, bless you!" he bellowed as he lifted my entire body up off of the floor and swung me back and forth in his king-sized hug. "You are so precious!"

To say I was taken aback would be the world's greatest understatement. I was floored. I was bewildered. I was shocked. I was totally not expecting whatever this was.

Joe charged forward. "They tell me your name is Hannah Hunter," he said. "I have a dream to change your name to Hannah Hardy. What do you think? If you want to keep Hunter, I'm totally fine with it. But, as far as I've seen, Hardy is the best last name starting with an H that's out there. And I'd love to share it with you."

I couldn't speak.

"Oh, no need to say anything right now," he said, recognizing I wasn't able to speak. "I'm guessing you're hungry, you're tired, and you're terrified by me roaring in here with my gigantic personality and squeezing you to death!"

I couldn't speak, but Monica could.

"Wait!" Monica said, standing up and pointing at Joe. "You're that adventure guy on TV, aren't you?"

"My name's Joe," he replied. "What's yours?"

"Monica Ableman — Hannah's social worker," she said.

"Monica, it's good to know you," he said with a huge smile. "I'm not on television anymore. That was my previous life. Now I'm just an ordinary guy that looks a lot like an adventure guy that used to be on television."

Monica was totally confused by this. But she smiled graciously.

Meanwhile, I was racking my brain trying to remember some adventure guy on television named Joe Hardy. I couldn't think of anyone that fit the bill. I had never seen this guy before in my life.

So from the beginning, Joe Hardy was never a celebrity in my eyes. He was always just an ordinary guy that looked a lot like a television adventure guy from which everyone always wanted an autograph.

Joe was warm. He was genuine. He was thoughtful. He was kind. He was handsome. He was even funny. But the quality that stood out in my mind, more than any other, was that he was also a threat of yet another rejection, yet another *Left* to tag onto my ever-growing list of *Lefts* to count.

Hannah Hannah Bobanna was still at large in my life. And even without Candy to collaborate with, she immediately went to work searching for a way to destroy this man and make him rue the day he'd decided to be kind to her.

Chapter Five

Chatting with Uncle Hal

Uncle Hal, per usual, had a grand solution for me. Here's how he presented it:

"Hannah baby," he crooned, "this strange Hardy man is preparing to reject you. You know that, don't you?"

"I know!" I agreed.

"You can't fall for his kindness and care," Hal said. "It's all part of the emotional setup. His game is to get you to trust him and then he lowers the boom and rejects you like last year's prom dress."

"I'm on to him," I said.

"But one more rejection, Hannah baby," he said, "would be too painful for your sensitive heart, so it's imperative that we protect you!"

"I can't handle another rejection, Uncle Hal!" I agreed with tears welling in my eyes. "I would die!"

"You're right!" He nodded understandingly, "you would keel over and breathe your last! You simply can't handle it!" Then he leaned in conspiratorially: "So here's what you do."

My soul moved close to hear the strategy.

"You must reject and destroy Joe Hardy before he rejects and destroys you," he said in grave seriousness. "*Capeesh?*"

"*Capeesh!*" I replied with a nod.

And the scene was set for the destruction of Joe Hardy — the guy dumb enough to think that he could play such a game with my heart and come out the other end in one piece.

Chapter Six

The Evil Plot

Here's how the plan to destroy Joe Hardy worked...

Step One: fake it.

To fake it, I can't allow him to know I'm scheming to destroy him. If he finds out, he could get the jump on me and destroy me first. You see, I'm aware he is scheming to destroy me, so I can't let on that I know that juicy tidbit of information. My job is to act like I'm happy being his daughter. That way I can hopefully get to him before he gets to me.

Step Two: bait him to trust me.

Joe's game is to bait me to trust him. So I'm turning the tables on him and baiting him to trust me. I want him to think that I'm trustworthy so that he will entrust me with all his critical data. I need to gather lockbox locations, lockbox keys, and lockbox codes. Then, when the moment is right, I can strike at his heart.

Step Three: lower the boom.

I can't wait too long to make my dastardly move. I can't be lulled to sleep by Joe's kindness and care. I must remain on my guard and look for the perfect moment to deliver the destructive blow. He must be totally shocked if this plan is going to work.

When I spray painted pink graffiti on the Carlisles' home, I felt something — something unusual. It was intense guilt. And I didn't like it one bit. And though I struggled to wiggle out of its forceful grip, I did eventually make it free. I didn't like the feeling of guilt, and I didn't like it when it started to creep back in as I worked on my evil plot against Joe Hardy.

The Carlisles were easier for me to hurt because they had wronged me. They had belittled me at times. They had spoken harshly towards me, criticized Candy, and even told me I was stupid. They supplied enough good reasons for me to justify my own horrid actions. But it wasn't the same with Joe Hardy.

Joe was different from anyone I had ever met. He was different from any of my social workers, any of my employers, any of my juvenile detention caseworkers, any of my friends, and any of my foster parents.

He was...amazing. And I mean that. I don't mean he was perfect, but he was so kind, so thoughtful towards me. And when he made a mistake, he would just come up to me and say, "Hannah, I'm so sorry that I did that."

You would think that I would have wanted this. And you'd be right. I did. But instead of being grateful, all Joe's niceness made me mad. After all, Uncle Hal had warned me about his kindness and care. He had convinced me it was a ruse. Joe Hardy was preparing to reject me. I needed to remember that — I needed to keep that at the forefront of my mind. The little girl in me craved what Joe was giving me — protection, love, kindness, sensitivity, care, and profound patience. But I couldn't fall for the bait.

I was convinced that Joe Hardy was attempting to draw

me into his spider web of niceness. He was setting me up to destroy me. I needed to tell myself every day, "Hannah, remember, you can't handle one more rejection."

Chapter Seven

September 12, 1985

This is the first time that I have written all this down. And to be frank, I'm really struggling right now. Seeing all of my evil antics written in black and white is horrifying to my soul. I can only imagine what all of you reading this will think of me as a result.

But the reason I'm writing this is not just to show how bad I was in the past, but how good God is at rescuing those of us that seem beyond the pale of rescue.

I've been sitting here at my computer for the past ten minutes wondering how to write down what happened on September 12, 1985. It's been almost nine years since that terrible day, and yet I still don't have words to describe it.

I am ashamed. I'm mortified by my actions. I'm repulsed by my behavior.

I plotted and planned to destroy the one person in my life that did *not* leave me — the one person in my life that was kind, caring, loving, and patient with me. I sabotaged the one person in my life that had a vision for what I could actually become. I attempted to punish him for daring to serve me.

After sitting here for another half hour staring out the window of my bedroom into the backyard, observing my children happily playing in our backyard sandbox, I've decided I can't write down the details. Because they don't matter. What matters is that you know I did something far worse to Joe than spray painting graffiti on the front of his house. I pulled the pin on a grenade and left town — tossing the bomb into his life and officially parting ways with the sweetest season I had ever known.

Who would do such a thing?

I did.

I did it. I did something so wrong that I just knew I could never be forgiven for it.

Chapter Eight

Letters from Joe

How would you expect Joe Hardy to respond to my actions?

I have an excerpt from my journal, dated September 25, 1985 which explains how I personally thought he would respond.

Joe will fall to pieces. I just know it. He will scream. He will beat his chest. He will declare that adopting me was the biggest mistake of his entire life. And he will hate me until the day he dies.

How wrong I was.

Joe didn't fall to pieces. He didn't scream. He didn't beat his chest. He didn't declare that adopting me was the biggest mistake of his entire life. And he didn't hate me until the day he died.

Instead, he did something that wholly shocked me. *He pursued me.*

Me. He pursued *me.* The girl who tried to destroy him and his reputation.

I wish I could say that this astounding response from Joe changed me, restored my sanity, and finally broke through my Uncle Hal–induced victim delusions in which I was imprisoned, but it didn't.

Joe discovered that I was in a safe house in Albuquerque, New Mexico. So he sent personal letters to every social service worker in the area. Each letter said the same thing:

> *If you know the whereabouts of a seventeen-year-old girl named Hannah Hunter Hardy, please deliver a message to her for me. Tell her that her father loves her heaps and heaps. Tell her that I want her to come home.*

A year later, Joe discovered that I was attending a community college in Las Cruces. He started sending letters addressed to me to the administration office.

"Hannah," they would say, "you received another letter."

"Burn it!" I would say.

I didn't even read them. I couldn't read them. Because every time I thought of what I had done, it brought back a wave of oppressive guilt. The only way I thought I could escape the guilt was to escape the memory of my terrible deed.

Three years later, Joe somehow discovered that I had moved to Wellington, Colorado. Letters started arriving at my apartment in alarming number.

On the outside it would say, "Please please open me" or "I love you, dear one" or "I'm still here loving you."

I wrote on the outside of every single one of them Return to Sender.

"Leave me alone!" I shouted one night as I walked through the door of my small apartment only to find yet another Joe Hardy letter waiting on the floor, having been slipped through the mail slot on my door.

"Leave me alone, Joe!" I shouted again.

Something about that particular letter started something inside me.

On the outside were the words "I'm not leaving you, Princess."

With the pile of mail in my trembling hands, I fell to my knees on the wood floor and wept. It was the first time I had allowed the soul trauma to come to the surface. I was there in a sobbing heap on the floor for probably an hour. The deep regret just bubbled out of me in waves.

It was a start. I still had a long way to go.

That next Sunday I stepped into a church building for the first time in four years. I had gone to church maybe fifteen times in my entire life and every one of those times was when I lived with Joe.

I guess, subconsciously, I was hoping to find someone like Joe there at the church. I realize that sounds strange, but I wanted Joe's love, his ever-present smile, and his contagious laugh in my life. I wanted to start over. I didn't want to hurt people anymore. I wanted to help people.

It may sound obvious that I could just call up Joe and apologize. I could just write a letter back that says, "I blew it. Please forgive me. I'm coming home if you will have me." But that option felt like a black hole of pending rejection. There was simply no way Joe Hardy could forgive me for what I did. Never mind that every letter was practically screaming that he had already forgiven me. It still felt impossible. So I would need to find the love and kindness of Joe Hardy elsewhere.

Maybe I could find it here in Wellington, I thought. Maybe I could find another super-kind, super-funny, super-loving, kind of gray-headed, dad-sort-of guy that

I could actually love back, be truthful towards, and bless instead of bludgeon.

I realize my logic was strange, but that is where the long trip home started.

It started on October 22, 1989 in Wellington Community Church.

I was trembling as I hopped out of my rusty little car and made my way to the front doors of the small church. As I opened those doors, it was my way of saying, "God, I want to come home. I really do. Could you accept this as my way of trying to make things right?"

The first person I met was Cathy Pfister, the pastor's wife. She looked at me and, without saying a word, walked up to me and hugged me.

I was completely bewildered and frozen stiff with fright. I needed that hug so desperately. I needed to know that God was welcoming. I needed to know that there was a bit of hope in this dark world. And Cathy Pfister's hug supplied that.

As she held me, I flashed back to meeting Joe for the first time. I remembered his warm hug.

Cathy held me for a long time. And while she was holding me she said something that I've never forgotten.

"You are welcome here, dearie," she said. "I don't know what troubles your life has thrown at you, but Jesus is ready to be your champion."

That's how it started. Right there, in Cathy's arms.

It was the first time I can say that Uncle Hal's appeals toward continuing as a victim sounded false. I was beginning to see through the victim sham.

Why? Because I just heard that I had a Champion. And that Champion was able to help save me from my troubles.

Chapter Nine

The Warm Blanket

I came to Wellington Community Church that day in October of 1989 hoping to find an alternate Joe Hardy. The real Joe Hardy could never again be my father and my friend. That ship had sailed. But, maybe, just maybe, I thought I could potentially atone for my sins by loving and caring for someone else that was cast in the Joe Hardy mold.

If you are thinking I was delusional, I wouldn't argue with you. But, in my Uncle Hal–clouded brain, this all somehow made a strange kind of sense.

Cathy invited me home for lunch after church. Liston, her husband and the pastor of the church, greeted me with a big smile at the door, and I thought, "Here he is! I just found another Joe Hardy."

The warmth of the Pfister home was like a soft blanket wrapping around my shoulders on a frigid winter day. It had been a long time since I had laughed — or smiled for that matter. That afternoon, something began to thaw inside me.

I wanted the joy that this couple had. I wanted the peace that their home enjoyed. I had tasted it briefly in

Joe Hardy's home, but I had rejected it before it could reject me first. Now, I found myself craving a second chance. I didn't want to ever lose this feeling.

Over the next eight weeks, it became a tradition to come over to Liston and Cathy's place after church for Sunday dinner. Every week they would invite me and another family. I began to feel a part of something. And if you could divide up friends into the category of good and bad — I was actually beginning to build friendships with people that had a good impact on my life.

On the seventeenth of December that same year, I headed over to the Pfisters per the usual custom. All was friendly, fun, and beautiful. And then, in the middle of our Sunday dinner, the front door opened and in walked a young man.

I wrote the following in my journal that afternoon when I returned home:

> *Something strange happened today. It was both magical and scary. It was both wonderful and dangerous. I just met a young man. He was kind to me. In fact, the first words he said to me were, "Oh, Hannah Hardy! My mom and dad keep telling me about you." I didn't know how to respond. I just stood there and stared. It was quite embarrassing. But he was such a gentleman. He made me feel at ease. He is always smiling. He is always ready to laugh. He is always aware of everyone around him and what they may be needing. My insides are trembling as I write this. I'm scared to think about him, but he's all that has filled my mind since I first laid eyes on him. His name is Adam. He's the Pfisters' youngest son, home from Bible College for Christmas break. He may not be the most handsome man I've ever seen, but he's a man that reminds me of Joe. And Joe is the best man I've ever met.*

Chapter Ten

My Little Joe

It's startling to admit to myself that what attracted me most to Adam was that he reminded me of Joe.

Adam was (and still is) exuberant, at times bigger than life. His smile filled a room. His social confidence was like wind beneath my wings. He was kind, thoughtful, and always patient. And he won my heart.

Adam ask me to marry him in the Pfister kitchen five months later. I had been taking cooking lessons from Carol. I was completely inexperienced when it came to all skills domestic and she had taken me under her wing and was investing everything she knew into me. That particular day she was teaching me how to bake homemade bread.

Adam was away at school, preparing to graduate. I was at home missing him something terrible.

I remember I was greasing a bread pan while chatting with Carol. Suddenly I realized Carol wasn't saying anything, so I looked up. Carol was no where to be seen. She had vanished.

Then the stereo turned on in the living room and soft piano music began to play. It was my favorite song, George Winston's *Joy*.

I was so confused. I was setting down my bread pan when, suddenly, Adam walked into the kitchen. His smile lit up the room.

I was dumbfounded, staring back in bewilderment. He was supposed to be at college. How did he get here? Where was Carol? She was supposed to be teaching me about baking bread. Why was there music playing?

Adam reached out and took my hand. It was trembling. Tears began to involuntarily bubble up in my eyes and flood down my cheeks.

He knelt in front of me and said these words:

"Miss Hardy, would you do me the honor of becoming my wife?"

Words wouldn't come out of my throat. So I nodded a very smiley, happy, tear-drenched nod.

When I floated home that evening after sharing a surreal festive dinner with the Pfister family, I found a letter from Adam waiting for me.

Let me share with you one of the paragraphs he wrote.

> *I know it's been difficult for you to trust. I know you have experienced a lot of pain. God specializes in new beginnings, Hannah. I believe strongly that if you trust Him with all those aches and pains, He will overwrite your tragedy with an amazing story of triumph.*

If you can believe it, I struggled to accept all this beauty in my life. I felt like God had mixed me up with some other Hannah, and I was receiving the rewards of her well-lived life. I thought that I probably needed to make some things clear to God.

"God," I said, "remember, I'm Hannah Hunter. I'm

the one who was so wicked, who spent an entire year of my life trying to destroy the life of innocent people. I'm the one who tried to ruin my adoptive father — the only person who ever gave me a chance. I don't deserve a good life. I deserve pain. Don't get me wrong, God. I don't want pain. But I feel terrible taking the blessings that belong to someone else."

There have been many truths that I have awakened to over the past five years that have totally altered my life. The idea that I could ever be lovable and desirable has likely been one of the most difficult ones to get through my thick head.

From the first moment I walked into Wellington Community Church and encountered the hug of Carol Pfister, I began a healing journey. And with every step forward on this healing journey, I felt my old life peeling away and a new life emerging. My fears subsided, my anger disappeared, and even my selfish obsessions melted away. I was new. Jesus Christ was changing me.

Adam kept reminding me of this change.

"Call your father," he would say. "You need to invite him to the wedding."

"I can't," I would reply.

"Why not?" he would ask.

I didn't have a good answer to that question.

Why not?

With all my growing clarity and growing maturity in seemingly every area of life, there was an emotional fog that lingered over the matter of Joe Hardy.

What I did to Joe was so extreme. And in my deepest center, it seemed unpardonable. What if I called him up and he said, "Hannah, I've been thinking a lot about what you did. Even though I wish I could forgive you, I can't — your sin was just too great."

That risk of a possible rejection from Joe was paralyzing to me.

I never did invite Joe to the wedding. That thought has haunted me ever since. I missed the opportunity to have him not just share in that precious day, but to walk me down the aisle.

I wanted it so badly. I wanted to have him be a part of my life. But there, deep inside my soul, were the lingering effects of Uncle Hal's Old Bearded Con Man Ruse. I was still counting from the *Left*.

Chapter Eleven

The Package

Three days before our wedding, a package arrived through FedEx. It was for me. And it was from Joe.

I gulped. Even seeing the package caused my emotions to swell and tears to flood my eyes.

I didn't know how he had found me. But, as Joe Hardy always did, he figured out my mailing address and had a message for me.

I had returned every single letter he had sent to me since the incident. Why would I open this one?

On the outside of the package were the words *Heaps and Heaps*.

That was Joe's phrase. He had said it a lot, always associating the phrase with his love and passion for his children.

It worked. I ripped open the box.

Inside was a video cassette with the words *Super Important!* written on it.

I popped the video into the video player and on the screen came my hero.

Always bigger than life, Joe Hardy was sitting in a chair looking just like he had five years earlier. He still was wearing that same fedora. He still had the gleam of joy twinkling in his eyes. And he still oozed that unique brand of love and kindness. He was staring into the camera and he said, "Hannah!"

I lost it. I began to sob.

How could Joe be smiling? How could he be so sweet? He was talking to me — the perpetrator of total evil — and he wasn't angry. He wasn't bitter. His words were so shockingly drenched in mercy and gentleness.

> *This is Dad on my Betamax camcorder. Every letter I have sent you has come back to me. I want you to know that I'm okay with that. But I'm trying something different here. Because I have something very important to share with you. I'm overnighting this package to you hoping that it is deemed interesting or important-looking enough to open. If you are watching this, then I guess my plan worked.*

I tried watching the screen but my tears blurred the picture. So I just closed my eyes and listened, letting his words wash over me like a hot shower.

> *I included a key in this package along with the cassette. It's a key to a bank lockbox at Wellington Bank just down the road from your new home. It's a wedding gift for you and your groom. I don't actually know his name. I just know it starts with the letter A. And I trust that he's a good man.*

The thought of Joe getting me a gift freshly overwhelmed me. And deep sobs followed. I actually paused the video. I sat there in front of my television for several minutes crying. Then, when I thought I could continue, I pushed play.

> *If you're ever in a dark place some day, I want you to remember what I'm about to tell you. You've always counted from the Left. Your birthparents left. Your Aunt Phyllis left. Your friends left. That's three Lefts. And you've been counting those Lefts a lot, haven't you? But I implore you, dear precious daughter of mine, to count from the Right. Your dad loves you heaps. Your dad really loves you heaps. Your dad really really loves you heaps and heaps. That's three Rights. There is a whole lot that is right in your life. I'm always here for you when you are ready to talk. And… congratulations. I'm so glad you're marrying a good man named… Alphonso? Abraham? Adonijah? Antwon? Agulagrimgobby? Am I getting close? Well, whatever his name is, if he's marrying you, it shows he has good taste. I know you are going to be happy.*

I can't actually tell you how many times I watched that video. Because I wasn't counting. It must have been upwards of fifty times. And every time I played it I would cry, then I would laugh, then I would cry, then I would laugh.

Joe should have been at my wedding. I realize that now. He should have been there for the birth of my little girl, Caroline. I see that clearly. And I should have reached out to him and sought forgiveness before he passed. I had so many opportunities. There are a lot of things I see clearly now, and yes, I really wish I had seen them earlier. But I'm choosing to celebrate the fact that I *do* see them now.

I still wear a necklace around my neck that Joe gave me as a wedding gift.

The inscription on it reads: Really Really Heaps and Heaps.

Chapter Twelve

Joe's Final Gift

Joe Hardy revealed my Heavenly Father to me.

He loved me even when I was unlovable.

He adopted me even when I was a mess.

He forgave me even when I did evil against Him.

He relentlessly pursued me, never giving up until I surrendered to His love.

When I think about God, I can't help but think about Joe. Maybe it's sacrilegious to say this, but to me, Jesus looks like Joe Hardy, fedora and all.

I don't deserve Jesus's love. But He gives it anyway.

I don't deserve Jesus's kindness. But He pours it out in extravagant abundance.

I don't deserve a second chance. But He gives me four hundred thousand chances (and still counting).

I received a telegram on September 6, 1991. This is what it said:

> *Mrs. Hannah Pfister,*
> *My name is Juanita Gomez. You may remember me. I've been your father's secretary for the past thirty-five years.*

I'm saddened to inform you that your father, Joe Hardy, passed away yesterday. As you could guess, he was adventuring when God took him home.

His memorial service is planned for Saturday, September 14th.

More than anything, Joe desired you to return home for his memorial service. I've purchased plane tickets for you already in hopes of making Joe's vision a reality. I am prepared to overnight them to you in the event that you give me the go-ahead.

Please let me know. My phone number is listed below.

He loved you very much, Hannah.

Sincerely,

Juanita Gomez

Adam forced me to go to the memorial. I have never been more scared than I was that day. I expected a bolt of lightning to strike me down. I expected everyone at the memorial to turn around in their chairs and boo me in unison. I expected rejection, but I received something very different.

I came to Joe Hardy's funeral and it seemed like he was awaiting my arrival with a bouquet of roses.

Mrs. Gomez hinted that I should go to his old house. When I arrived at the home, there was another clue encouraging me to head to a nearby cave. And in the cave there was yet another clue, and then another, and another. Each clue revealed my father's amazing love for me, his extraordinary and inexplicable forgiveness, his exquisite mercy, and his undying enthusiasm for my life.

At every turn in this dark cave the lights turned on in my soul. I saw the lies I had believed and I saw the truth I had shunned. And in the end, there awaited me a priceless gift from my dear father.

Before he had died, Joe spent hundreds of hours building the ultimate expression of paternal love and care for me. It was a treasure hunt that led me to a deep and profound understanding of not just Joe's love for me, but God's love for me.

Chapter Thirteen

Surrounded on the 405

When I think of O. J. Simpson in his white Ford Bronco driving down the 405 refusing to yield to the police — I think of me.

It's such a ridiculous thing to flee from God, from truth, from responsibility. But how often have I done it?

Every one of the ninety-five million folks watching Simpson's slow-speed chase down the 405 freeway knew that it was a foregone conclusion that O. J. would eventually be caught. So why did he keep going? What was the purpose of that two-hour escapade?

For that matter, what was the purpose of my twenty-year escapade? Why did I fight something so wonderful from taking place in my life? Why did I run from joy, from love, and from peace?

It's truly insanity.

Even when I was a filthy, self-absorbed, hateful sinner, Joe wanted me.

And even when I spat back in the face of his love,

kindness, mercy, and patience, Joe forgave me.

Joe never gave up.

And he was only a miniature representation of the One who was really after me the entire while, chasing me down the 405 freeway of my life.

I praise God that He never stopped chasing me as I attempted to escape in my own personal white Ford Bronco.

He finally got me to pull my vehicle over to the side of the road and step out of my rebellion and into His mercy.

I have been arrested by His love. And I feel that is the perfect place to be. I want to remain in this place forever.

Chapter Fourteen

Counting from the Right

I'm happy to say that I don't count from the *Left* any more. Uncle Hal's shenanigans no longer work on me. Instead, I have begun to count from the *Right*.

I have so many things that are *Right* in my life.

I have a husband who is a true prince.

I have two little kiddos who are daily reminders of God's beauty.

I have two in-laws who love me like a daughter and treat me like royalty.

I have three Hardy siblings who have become my best friends.

I have a church community that gives me a taste of heaven.

I have a little house in Wellington that to me is a palace of peace.

I have a Savior who refused to give up on me, and gave up everything to redeem me.

And I can see all this *Right* because I had a father named

Joe Hardy who broke through my selfish fog, endured my calloused heart, was pierced by my stupidity, and really really loved me heaps and heaps.

www.ingramcontent.com/pod-product-compliance
Lightning Source LLC
Chambersburg PA
CBHW061843040426

42447CB00012B/3106